A MOTHER'S MANUAL

A MOTHER'S MANUAL

Darlene Brooks

Darlene Brooks
2075 Seventh Avenue Suite #3
New York, NY 10027
www.amothersmanual.com
Publisher's note: This is a work of nonfiction. Names, characters, places, and incidents are a product of the author's imagination. Locales and public names are sometimes used for atmospheric purposes. Any resemblance to actual people, living or dead, or to businesses, companies, events, institutions, or locales is completely coincidental.
Book layout © 2015 createspace.com
Cover illustration by Hilary Dunne
Library of Congress Copyright Registration due upon request

A Mother's Manual / Darlene Brooks.
First edition
ISBN-13: 9781517683856
ISBN-10: 1517683858
Library of Congress Control Number: 2016904133
CreateSpace Independent Publishing Platform
North Charleston, South Carolina

To Perry, Crystal, Bianca, and Treasure
My children—my inspiration to be better.

You don't have to be a perfect parent.
Do be a present parent.
Fight through adversity. Change what you need to.
Change the world.
--Darlene Brooks

FOREWORD

As THE REST of my friends exited to meet their parents for pictures, I remained behind. I sat on the bathtub in my evening gown, fixated on my image in the yellow-tinted bathroom mirror. The high cheekbones and large brown eyes adorning my face were vaguely reminiscent of someone I couldn't quite grasp. My gaze pierced my reflection, searching my visage for that person to whom it appeared I was identical. Still entranced by the eerie feeling that I had seen a ghost, I reapplied my lip gloss and left the bathroom. Downstairs was a grouping of adults, cameras clutched in each of their hands like precious jewels. My friends and I stood in inorganic poses, speaking to one another through permanent smiles situated on our faces. Flashes from Androids and iPhones jolted about the room when an older woman stopped to inquire my name. I introduced myself to her, simultaneously grabbing the attention of the other mothers I had yet to meet. Seeing that it was a senior prom, and I—a sophomore—was attending as a guest of a friend, only a few parents present knew me. The women began to pick and prod at my hair, nails, and dress. They showered me with compliments and praised my elegance. One woman exclaimed, "If you're this gorgeous, I wonder what your mother looks like!" That's when another adult, a friend of my mom, replied, "When you look at her, you are looking at her mother!"

As I venture further into young adulthood and pursue my passion of activism and helping others, I am constantly reminded of how my mother has molded me into a respectable person. Whenever I find myself aiding another human being or cultivating the life of another, I notice my hands callusing in all the same places as hers, something I consider a true badge of honor. Just as I was taught as a child, this book is written simplistically so that a larger audience may comprehend the profound lessons. The messages are articulated in concise, thoughtful passages that speak to mothers of all racial, socioeconomic, religious, political, and educational backgrounds. The wisdom bound within these pages is an accumulation of my mother's trial and error after raising four children— all of whom work to be positive reflections of the woman we know as "Mommy." As an avid reader, there are two questions I ask myself to determine if what I've read was a good book: The first is whether I am the same person I was before reading the book; if the answer is yes, the author has failed. The second is whether I had a willingness to change before reading the book; if the answer is no, then I have failed. If you are looking for reassurance that raising successful children is easy, then I regretfully inform you that this is not in fact the book for you. If you are picking up this book with the same eagerness to learn as you had when first entering motherhood, then it's about time you turn the page. Welcome to *A Mother's Manual.*

Treasure Brooks

PREFACE

When I was in my 20's I am sure I was considered least likely to ever have any children.

I have always been an adventurer, a free-spirit. People constantly ask me how I raised such accomplished children. The compliment I get most is that I am an amazing mother. I was blessed to have four wonderful children. I *decided* to become a mother. I gave it serious and conscious consideration. I chose to devote most of my time and energy into raising my children to be the best they could be. When I thought about my life's purpose, I thought about my children. I believe my purpose is directly related to being a mother. When I look at their strength and continued growth and even making history in their chosen endeavors, I know I did many things right. That's when I began writing the passages for A Mother's Manual.

Did I have any idea of the additional challenges I would face during the process? Absolutely not! No one foresees two divorces, homelessness, unemployment, a domestic violence shelter, foreclosure, surgery, paralysis, more surgery, etc. all occurring while trying to raise healthy children. Most women are usually unaware of the many changes and challenges they will encounter after giving birth. I want to convey the idea, especially to young women, that having a baby is not the same as entering motherhood. Just as having a wedding is not the same as entering into a marriage. As an experienced mother, I am able to assist by giving pointers that I have used to raise responsible, intelligent, compassionate and productive children. I want to encourage mothers from all walks of life to keep a laser focus on their children, come what may, from birth and continually through their adult lives. By strengthening and reinforcing the role of mother, children will flourish in their true calling. I would like to see a reduction in neglected, abandoned and abused children, juvenile crime rates, premature pregnancies, high school dropouts and dysfunctional families. I am not trying to discourage women from having children. Rather, I am trying to encourage them to equip themselves with the strength and patience that they will need to withstand the task.

The things I endured after I had my children were so difficult sometimes, that only my life experience, a spiritual awakening to who I was and wanted to be and my hopes for my children, kept me sane. Overcoming each obstacle helped me to never take lightly my responsibilities as a mother.

What I did realize throughout my obstacles was that my children's future was at stake and they had to come first. Everything I faced, they experienced. That just made me more determined and more focused on their well-being. I never made excuses, I just did whatever was necessary to keep them thriving. Today my son is a University of California graduate. I have daughters attending both a Historically Black university and an Ivy League university. My youngest is on her path to great things at a prestigious private high school. In their own right they have made world news, traveled extensively around the globe, mentored other children and continue to be world-changers. All I ever asked is that they "do not consume and complain, but work to make the world better, no matter what profession they might choose."

Writing this book, "A Mother's Manual" is a testament to my purpose. When I began writing the passages for the book, my children were in elementary, middle, high school and college. I have continued to simultaneously deal with every stage of child-rearing. The teaching and learning for both myself and my children is ongoing. I have included every important aspect of parenting that I have personally experienced.

A Mother's Manual is my gift to mothers and parents because we all want the best for our children. I believe motherhood is the greatest purpose any woman can choose. It is the most demanding, sacrificial and important job that exists. There is no greater joy than seeing your children healthy, happy and succeeding in life. Mothers shape the world we live in simply by the way we raise our children. It is often said that raising children does not come with an instruction manual. Now, it does.

Darlene Brooks

INTRODUCTION BY BIANCA BROOKS

I HAD A close relationship with my literature teacher, Ms. Joe, when I was in 10th grade. What connected us was our love of words, but what sustained us was her investment in my budding womanhood. During lunch I would seek refuge in Ms. Joe's classroom, where I would share with her my latest revelations about life or discuss the whatever book I was reading at the time. I distinctly recall running to her one afternoon to relay an argument I had with my mother the night before over some sort of teen-angst "she just doesn't get it" type problem. I will never forget how Ms. Joe told me to retell the story, but insisted that I replace all the times I said "mom" with my mother's name, Darlene. I began to retell the story, but immediately found that I had made unrealistic demands of my mother, who, in that moment, I realized was a whole human being who was simply trying to understand me as another whole human being.

I tell this story to say that learning what it is to be a mother is so much more than reading a book or taking a Lamaze class. Learning to be a mother is a constant lesson in understanding--- understanding what it means to be a daughter, a friend, a teacher, a student...a person. When we take on the task of donning the title of these sacred roles, it becomes easy to forget that we are still developing ourselves as individuals apart from who we are in relation to the ones we love. The greatest gift my mother ever gave me as a daughter, and continues to give me, was permission to be myself. On the seventh day of October of 1996, she named me Bianca. But from that day onward, she has allowed me to decide exactly what that means. Mothers do not *make* children any more than seeds make flowers or garages make cars. Mothers give life to children, and give space for those children to become whoever it is they become. It is a continual gift and a perpetual honor to be a mother--- a daughter, a sister, a teacher, a student, a friend.

This book is as much about honor as it is about anything else. This book is about partaking in the sacred ritual of gift-giving, every day, for all time. Motherhood is an occasion you rise to. And though this book will begin to both prepare you for the occasion and prepare you to give that gift, it could never adequately express what it will mean for your children to receive it. What you are about to read is not just a how-to manual; it is a testament to the gift my mother has given me every single day of her life. This book bears witness to all she has ever done for me as both a mother and as Darlene. The result of this book, my life and the lives of my siblings, is an attempt to return that gift, though always in a haphazard and less graceful manner than she has employed. Though I hope my daughterhood and womanhood (and eventual motherhood) is an adequate display of thanks for that gift, if not, I will simply say here-- Darlene, my mother, a million times thank you for rising to the occasion. I am who I am because you are who you are. And you are something special.

"A man came to the Prophet and said, 'O Messenger of God! Who among the people is the worthiest of my good companionship? The Prophet said: Your mother. The man said, 'Then who?' The Prophet said: Then your mother. The man further asked, 'Then who?' The Prophet said: Then your mother. The man asked again, 'Then who?' The Prophet said: Your father"

-Islamic Proverb

A Mother's Manual

Darlene Brooks

amothersmanual.com

Say the words
"I love you"
to your children,
every chance you get.

These simple, yet powerful
three words,
serve as food and music for
their soul—
and can never be heard too
much.

Hug and kiss your children often, no matter how old they are.

Such displays of affection are not only comforting and necessary, these are two of the best ways to express your love for them.

Teach your children to speak, read, write & count... *before* they start school.

You are their first teacher and home is their first school.

Participate with enthusiasm in your child's learning and education.

Your encouragement, attention and help with homework, studying and projects will help your child be a better student.

Guard your children from criminal, illicit or immoral people, and environments.

Many children are influenced or harmed daily by such exposure.

Teach your child how to be an active listener.

Listening is the most important part of communication.

Explore various ways to identify your child's gifts and talents.

This will help you to discover and cultivate your child's potential in their particular areas of talent.

Teach your children the importance of deciphering right from wrong.

This will help them to consider their actions before they act—and make good, fair and correct decisions.

Teach your children to apologize, with sincerity and remorse when necessary.

An apology begins the healing process and demonstrates compassion.

Do not refer to your children
negatively.
Be mindful of the words you speak
to and
about your children.

*Your words are very
powerful and can create
emotional scars that
sometimes never heal.*

Acknowledge &
compliment
your child's
unique physical
attributes (eyes,
smile, hair, legs,
etc.).

*Your compliments will help
to strengthen self-esteem
and instill confidence in
their appearance.*

Teach your children to be cooperative.

Being cooperative helps to reduce conflict and is one of the keys to working well with others.

Instill honesty in your child.

Honesty is not only the best policy; it is central to gaining and maintaining trust.

Teach your children not to be jealous or envious.

These feelings can breed resentment, improper behavior and even hate.

Teach your children to share.

Sharing is important to all relationships; and it helps to create a generous, giving spirit.

Teach your children the importance of being considerate.

Being considerate is part of the ethical code that will enable them to consistently act in a manner that is fair to others.

Recognize, compliment, celebrate, and reward your child's achievements.

This will serve as rocket fuel for your child to soar confidently through life.

Build and constantly reinforce strong self-esteem in your children.

Self-esteem is a key component of success and is central to everything: behavior, thoughts, and how they value themselves.

Teach your child to be unselfish.

Unselfishness is linked to selflessness, love, kindness, and fairness—all of which are essential to full character development.

Allow your children to cry when they feel the need to.

Tears can be a healing source for stress, pressure, and pain.

Be keenly aware of your children's emotional state (pain, depression, sadness, or confusion).

Such awareness will allow you to step in with love & understanding to comfort and give them the help they need.

Practice emotional stability, especially when your child is present.

Your child can feel all of your peace, happiness, and laughter—as well as your tension, anger, and sadness.

Always remember to be your child's best role model.

This is one of your main responsibilities. Your actions, along with your behavior and deeds, should be their example to follow.

Discourage your child from blaming others when your child is at fault.

Owning and accepting responsibility is the only way to do better, and is an important part of building good character.

Establish and enforce boundaries with your children.

This will enable them to accept "no" and respect certain limits that exist in life.

Do not give your children more material things than time, attention, and affection.

Things are not love and can cause a distorted sense of what is more valuable.

Attend your child's performances, games, and recitals.

Your presence in the audience makes your child feel appreciated and supported.

Never compare your children to their siblings in a negative manner.

This kind of comparing can damage confidence, cause sibling rivalries, and lead to resentment.

Teach your children the strength and virtue of patience.

Thinking before they act and waiting on processes will allow for control over emotions so that they may think rationally and act appropriately.

Teach your children how to focus.

Focus is the key to organization, task completion, skill mastery, and self-control.

Continually reinforce the important attribute of respect in your children.

Respect is a moral requirement that ensures the proper regard for everyone and everything.

Teach your children the importance of following rules and laws.

Not adhering to rules and laws can cause unnecessary setbacks and prevent them from advancing.

Teach your children about God, and show them how to pray & talk to God.

God is our ultimate source of life, wisdom, and strength—He is always there to listen, lead, and guide.

Help your child to understand death, and seek grief counseling when death affects your child.

Death is an inevitable part of life, and the grief it causes can have long-lasting effects.

Explain, explore, and discuss your children's heritage, cultural background, and history.

Cultural awareness will give them a better sense of who they are, instill pride, and help them create an effective road map for their futures.

Encourage your children to appreciate art and to express themselves artistically.

Art (drawing, painting, music, dance, sewing, writing) is an important and creative outlet to express thoughts and soothe their souls.

Teach your child to always act with compassion.

Compassion demonstrates a genuine concern for others and is one of the most important human character traits one can have.

Never discipline your children in the heat of your anger.

Anger is one letter short of danger! Disciplining while being angry can lead to irrational and excessive punishment, which is not only ineffective but also abusive.

Teach your children how to be still, quiet, and at peace.

This will help instill discipline and help them master self-control.

Make sure your children are not only physically healthy but mentally & spiritually healthy as well.

These are important elements of nurturing that ensure their complete health and wellness.

Create an attitude of gratitude in your children.

Gratitude allows them to have a heart of appreciation, which unlocks the door to living a more abundant life.

Always make chores part of a child's routine.

Doing chores will increase a sense of responsibility and earning as well as reduce any potential sense of entitlement.

Get to know your child's teachers & administrators, and attend school conferences and events.

Your involvement and interest in your child's education and your presence at his or her school will help your child excel.

Teach your children the importance of personal cleanliness, neatness, and good hygiene.

Personal maintenance is important to their overall physical health and self-image and contributes to how they are received by others.

Teach your children to always have respect for their elders.

Respecting their elders is a moral requirement that they will appreciate when they become elderly.

Teach your children to respect authority.

Respecting authority is a societal duty that will help keep them out of trouble.

Instill strong ethical behavior in your children.

Ethics is the link to morality, fairness, decision making, and the proper treatment of others.

Discuss news, world affairs, politics, laws, and government processes with your children.

Knowledge and interest in world systems help children to know what affects their lives and how to participate in change and progress.

Teach your children to be considerate of others' needs as well as their own.

Being considerate is linked to respect, regard, and fairness toward others and makes it easier to do the right thing in every situation.

Encourage your children to always dream and reach for their goals.

It is the dream that allows them to conceive...it is the plan that enables them to achieve.

Teach your children to be accountable for their actions and behavior.

Accountability is the first step to owning and accepting responsibility, which is essential to making corrections and positive changes.

Make sure that your children always maintain respectable language and behavior.

These are important boundaries to prevent disrespect, rudeness, and offensiveness.

Teach your children to be reliable.

This will make them trustworthy and dependable.

Always check up on your children's progress and development.

This will ensure they are receiving and doing what is best for them at each stage and level of their lives.

When your child demonstrates maturity and earns your trust, grant him or her certain freedoms.

Extending earned privileges shows your trust in your child's judgment and is an important part of the continued maturation process.

Do not always expect perfection from your child.

Remember, no one is perfect—and everyone goes through peaks & valleys when it comes to performance.

Teach your children the essentials of good manners.

Please, thank you, and excuse me - *among others, are important expressions that convey respect for others.*

Teach your children not to lie or deliberately deceive.

Lying and deception destroy trust & credibility—and could lead to immoral or illegal acts.

Always express to your children the importance of treating people the way they would like to be treated.

This is the Golden Rule—one of the most important rules and part of the ethical order; it serves as an important filter to all behavior.

Let your children know the benefits of learning new things in school and in life.

Learning stimulates and increases brain function, motivates them to explore, and enhances their creative abilities.

Teach your children the necessity of sacrifice.

Sacrifice is not only the ultimate demonstration of selflessness but also the center of such elements as unselfishness, love, and achievement.

Teach your child to be a civic-minded citizen.

Feelings of responsibility and taking action are essential to development, progress, and change in the local, national, and global communities.

Exhibit the image, class, style, and behavior that you would like your children to display.

They take their cues from you—and you are and should be your children's best role model.

Get to know the parents of your children's friends.

This will give insight on how your child will be cared for while visiting them.

Monitor the various forms of media that your child is exposed to.

Music, the internet, television, films, and games can be violent, hateful, and negative. Consuming such content often produces like behavior, thoughts, and attitudes.

Build strong self-respect in your children.

Strong self-respect allows them to fully love themselves—it guides their actions, behavior, and habits, as well as how they allow themselves to be treated by others.

Spend time with the friends or peers of your children.

Knowing their friends will give insight on potential influences, because peer pressure can play a major role in your children's decision making and behavior.

Teach your children the importance of dedication.

Dedication is the key that will unlock the door to personal achievement and excellence.

Help your children understand commitment.

Fulfilling obligations, keeping promises, respecting vows, and being loyal are necessary, honorable, and important character traits.

Instill the important principle of morality in your children.

Moral character will enable them to distinguish between right and wrong and to exercise good judgment.

Teach your children the value of identifying and learning from their mistakes.

Their mistakes are less likely to be repeated once they understand where they were in error, and their lesson is learned.

Teach your children the importance of teamwork.

Teamwork creates harmony and is vital to success and working well with others; it is required in school, at work, and in all relationships.

Teach your child how to make peace in times of disagreement.

Resolving conflict and being a peacemaker is a crucial life skill to have.

Discourage your children from participating in gossip and spreading rumors.

Gossiping and spreading rumors— whether true or not—is destructive, ruins reputations, and can negatively affect how people are viewed.

Make sure your child is aware of his or her own value and self-worth.

It is important that your child knows his or her life and existence has great purpose and significance.

Teach your child to be understanding.

Being understanding shows caring, compassion, and empathy. It is a trait that strengthens all relationships.

Frequently offer your child one-on-one time with you.

Spending time alone with your child shows him or her how important he or she is to you; it strengthens the bond and is another way to say "I love you."

Make sure you are not hypocritical and that your actions are consistent with your words.

Being consistent and leading by example will prevent hypocrisy, which can destroy your credibility.

Teach your children to have tolerance for others.

Tolerance is a human virtue that is necessary in a diverse world comprised of a multitude of many different kinds of people.

Identify the personality traits in your children that are inherited from you as well as those from their father.

Understanding your children's genetic traits will help you to better understand their personalities and their behavior.

Do not let your child be a witness to your anger or to you speaking badly about his or her father.

Speaking badly or belittling your child's father makes your child feel torn and can affect your child's self-esteem permanently because children see themselves as half of each parent.

Do not allow your issues, fears, and phobias to be passed on to your children.

Transferring fear or other issues can stagnate and inhibit them from freely experiencing life in their own right.

Listen to your children.

Listening will allow you to respond appropriately and understand them better, and it will help strengthen the bond between you.

Be open with your children about changes in your circumstances (health, finances, etc.).

Your circumstances will affect them, so they should be appropriately explained.

If you don't want your children to smoke, drink alcohol excessively, or use drugs...

Don't you do these things. Remember, you are their role model.

Teach your children not to deliberately cause disturbances or pain to people, animals, or any living thing.

Such improper behavior illustrates a lack of regard and can lead to cruelty and abusive behavior.

Be understanding when your children make mistakes.

Making mistakes is a natural part of the growth and learning process. You do. You have. You will. As will they.

Teach your children to respect the property of others.

Respecting what does not belong to them shows respect for others. This includes avoiding the misuse, abuse, handling, or taking of anything without permission.

Explain karma to your children: "What goes around comes around."

What is given...is returned. There is absolutely no way around the law of reciprocity.

Instill a forgiving nature in your children.

Holding a grudge is a heavy weight that is counterproductive and will prevent them from moving forward.

Teach your children the importance of integrity.

Integrity is a vital quality that is linked to trust, honesty, and morality.

Teach your children the necessity of welcoming constructive criticism.

Honest and fair assessment is meant for their growth, improvement, and overall development.

Show your children how simple acts of kindness go a long way.

Sometimes the smallest display of kindness can make a big impact on someone's life.

Instill self-discipline in your children.

Self-discipline is an important pillar of success that enables one to stay focused and free from distractions.

Encourage your children to express their ideas no matter how unusual or unpopular their ideas may seem.

Innovations, new discoveries, and solutions are realized when the imagination is explored.

Teach your child how to grasp, clarify, and understand.

Understanding is how one learns; it also appropriately guides one's responses and interactions.

Teach your children mindfulness.

Being mindful, aware, and present in thoughts and feelings increases happiness and reduces anxiety and stress.

Develop leadership qualities in your children.

Being able to lead will afford them the opportunity to accomplish more in life and the ability to help others grow.

Teach your children the importance of being kind in their acts and their words.

Kindness makes others feel good and respected.

Listen to your children in certain situations without inserting feedback.

Sometimes, refraining from feedback or response allows you to fully hear them. And sometimes they just need you to listen.

Allow your child room to grow up and gain independence.

This prepares you and your child for the process of separation.

Introduce your children to your friends and other adults you think would serve as a good influence.

Children need exposure to people who can inspire and ignite their curiosity and help mentor them when needed.

Explain the power of unity to your children.

Coming together in one accord with others from different backgrounds promotes commonality, solidarity, and teamwork.

Involve your children in various social, community, and cultural activities.

This kind of enrichment and exposure enhances their social skills and helps to develop well-rounded, informed, and interesting people.

Teach your children to be humanitarians and engage in the caring and improvement of others' lives.

Humanitarians affect change concerning the welfare and well-being of the entire human race.

Teach your children how to earn, save, invest, and spend money wisely.

Knowing how to use money will help them understand the value of the dollar and maintain a financially secure lifestyle.

Show your children how to buy, prepare, and eat nutritious food and meals.

Eating the right food is key to being healthy and living a long life.

Make physical fitness a regular part of your child's routine.

Physical activity & exercise are necessary for preventing illness and disease.

Teach and show your children the importance of creating, maintaining, and participating in healthy relationships.

Healthy and positive relationships are crucial for a good life that is free of emotional pain, negativity, drama, and dysfunction.

Allow your children to know & love their father...no matter how you feel about him.

Children should be allowed to decide their own feelings about their father—intentionally restricting this process can cause an unnecessary void, a lifetime of damage, and emotional pain for your children.

Be willing to admit fault to your child when you make wrong choices for them.

Being able to own and admit missteps is the kind of humility that will allow you to make corrections and better choices in the future.

Explain to your children about the freedom and power of choice.

Help them to understand how the choices they make will also create the life they live.

Instill in your children the importance of having unshakeable faith and never-ending hope.

Faith is belief and an expression of hope for something better. Having faith and hope will give them a reason to move forward in spite of any and all circumstances life may bring.

Always be vigilant with your children—be ever-present & available. Never be too tired or too busy.

Such attentiveness not only keeps them safe but also is vital to how well they do in school, extracurricular activities, and in life.

Always tell and demonstrate to your children that you have high hopes for them.

Your constant encouragement and belief in them strengthens their confidence.

Teach your child to always be open to your correction.

You will always be your child's mother; he or she will never be too old for your guidance, wisdom, advice & correction.

Pace yourself: You will always be a mother. Your job will be ever-changing—but never-ending.

If you miss something, go back & repair, even if it's hard and takes a long time. Your children will always need your guidance, care, attention, and love— no matter how old they get.

ACKNOWLEDGMENTS

THANKS TO GOD and <u>all</u> my friends & family for being "The Village" that helped me to be the best mother I could be. I love you.

Anthony Family – for creating a wonderful loving circle of structure, support & fun for my family

Brother Roosevelt – for taking care of a very ill sister until she could stand and walk again

Charles O. S. – for being a supportive, encouraging and loving friend for decades and one who never stopped believing

Clara – for being nana and a beautiful, praying gift to us from God

Derreck – for being a support to your young cousin at Fisk U & an inspiration to your family

Dorothy – for being my mother and giving me everything you had to give me that made me who I am

GOMW/AF – for being a Godfather and giving us Africa, lessons and love from a King who cares

Gregory E D – for your patience. guiding and help to push me to finish this book, repeatedly nursing me back to health and especially, your true love and friendship. 143G

JB – for 3 beautiful daughters and a very hard time that only made me stronger

John B – for telling me "the attacks may not be about you; it may be a ploy to keep your children from seeing their destiny". That was priceless and so is your friendship

Kendall – for being a true friend & an attorney who always has the answers and a smile

Kyle – for supporting your young cousin's education and being a great example

Leroy – for being the kindest, caring friend & neighbor and helping a family in need

Linda D- for being a big sister, angel helper to a college kid in need and always just a prayer away

Lucky – for always smiling, and helping our family when I didn't have to ask

Masters School Community– for being the best school in the world and a blessing to my child

Napata – for your wisdom, laughs, love, cooking, music and sisterhood

Nicole – for your fun, friendship and instant genius in a pinch

Perry, Sr. – for our beautiful & brilliant son, loving and caring for me and my daughters always. Mostly, for showing me unconditional support, nonjudgement and love since the day we met

Randi N. – for being the best pediatrician and family friend

Sadie – for being my grandmother who knew what a grandmother is supposed to be

Shaw Family – for being the BEST family

Sherman Earl – for 30+ years of being my best friend, my ticket around the globe, my brother. You are my gift from God wrapped in everything I love!

Sister Teri – for praying with me, for me

Sisterfriends - Andria, Kim C, Kim M, Kim S, Mona, Sharon M -- for laughs, decades of love and support

Tanya/TMG, Esq. - for being wonderful Mama Tanya to my girls

Tony D – for being a classic man, an angel giver when I needed it most, for your words & music

Uncle Randy – for all my life being there for me, my big brother, believing in, loving & encouraging me

Wilson Family – for being my first family, protecting, providing and loving always

ABOUT THE ARTIST

AWARD-WINNING ARTIST **HILARY DUNNE** was born in Northamptonshire in England and has lived most of her life in or near to London. She has travelled extensively, particularly in Ethiopia where she has family connec-  tions, and in other parts of Africa, as well as in Indian, Latin America and the Caribbean. All of this has had a great influence on her life and painting.

Although always seriously interested in drawing and painting, when she left school, Hilary went on to study law at Nottingham University and in London. She practiced law in London, both as a partner in a large City practice and in a large financial institution, but eventually decided to move away from the law to enable herself to have more time to devote to painting. Largely self-taught as an artist, Hilary attended part time courses at Heatherleys and Central Saint Martins' Schools of Art in London to give herself a small part of the basic grounding she would have had from a fine art training. She has also studied mosaic in Ravenna, Italy, and at the Hampstead School of Art and the City Lit in London. Hilary's work has been used in television and theatre sets including the BBC2 television serial "Attachments", "Master Chef", again for BBC2 and in Nippon, Japan television's London program. In November 2014 Hilary was awarded the prestigious Meynell Fenton Prize at the ING Discerning Eye Exhibition at the Mall Galleries in London.

Hilary has now moved to a small village near to the historic town of Stamford where she works in an artistic community. She has a studio at her home which is open annually in June. The cover art, *Mother and Child*, is from an original painting by Hilary Dunne.

ABOUT THE AUTHOR

DARLENE BROOKS IS a parent coach, mentor, and motivational speaker—and a loving mother to four wonderful children. Though she has achieved success in the worlds of politics, sports, and entertainment, she considers motherhood her greatest accomplishment in life and wrote the book *A Mother's Manual* to help encourage and uplift other moms to become the best parents they can be.

As a media consultant and public relations professional, Brooks has lived and worked in Los Angeles; New York; Chicago; Washington, DC; and Atlanta. A certified crisis counselor and ordained minister, she currently resides in New York's beautiful Hudson Valley, though she regularly travels the world to volunteer for causes benefitting women, children, and individuals dealing with domestic abuse

Made in the USA
Columbia, SC
02 October 2020